SPOOKY & SCARY

Adult Coloring Book

I0502482

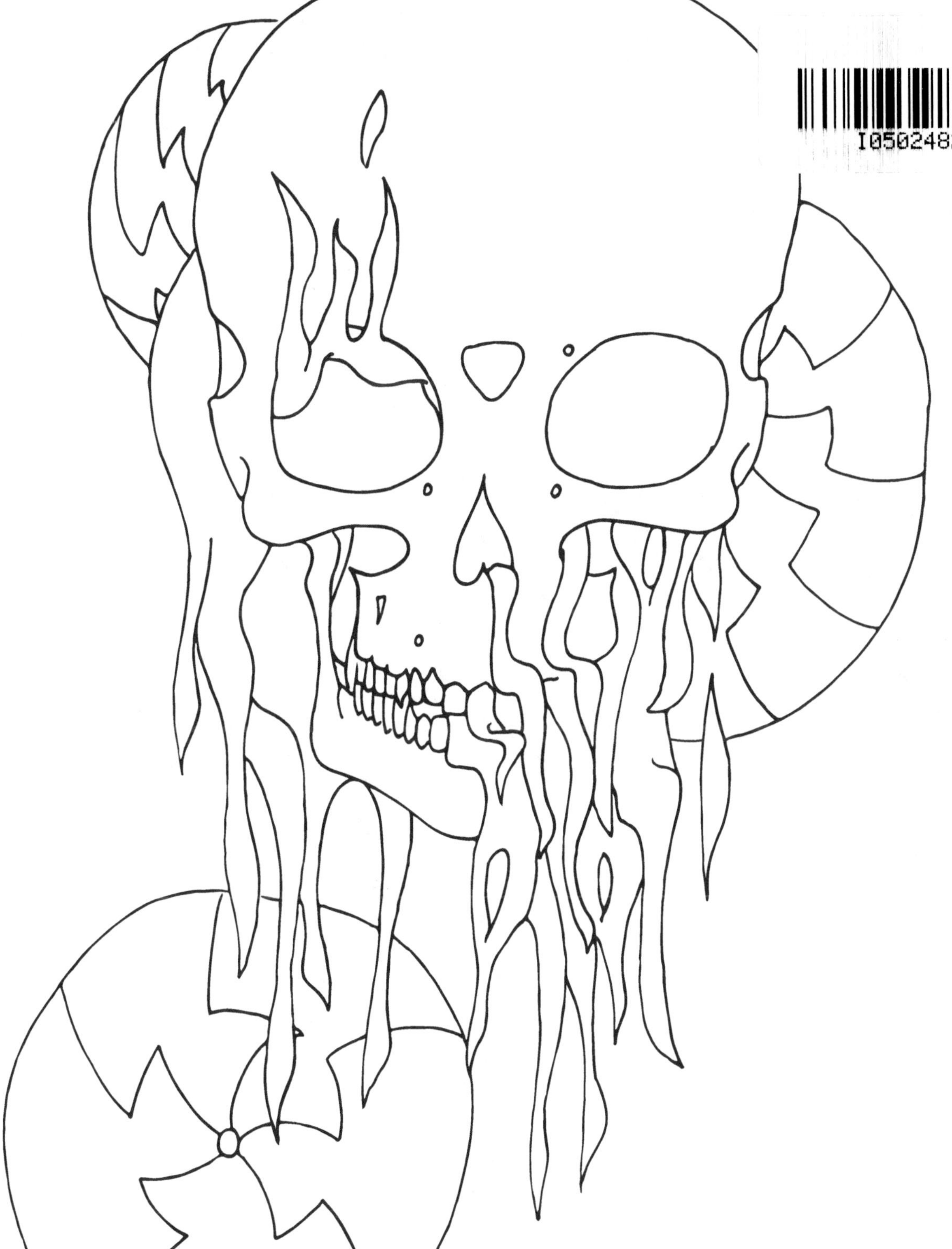

Jesse Stogianis

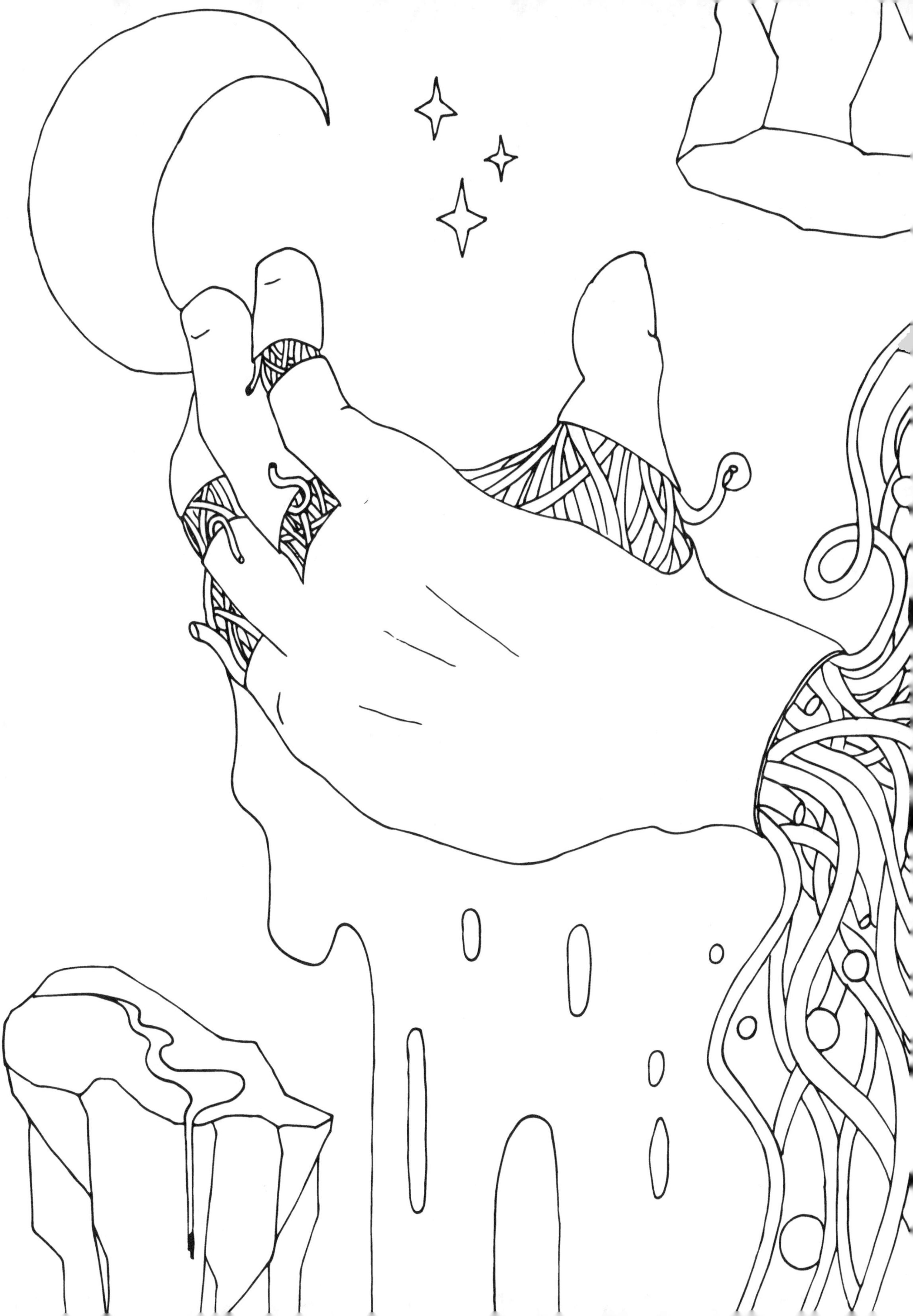

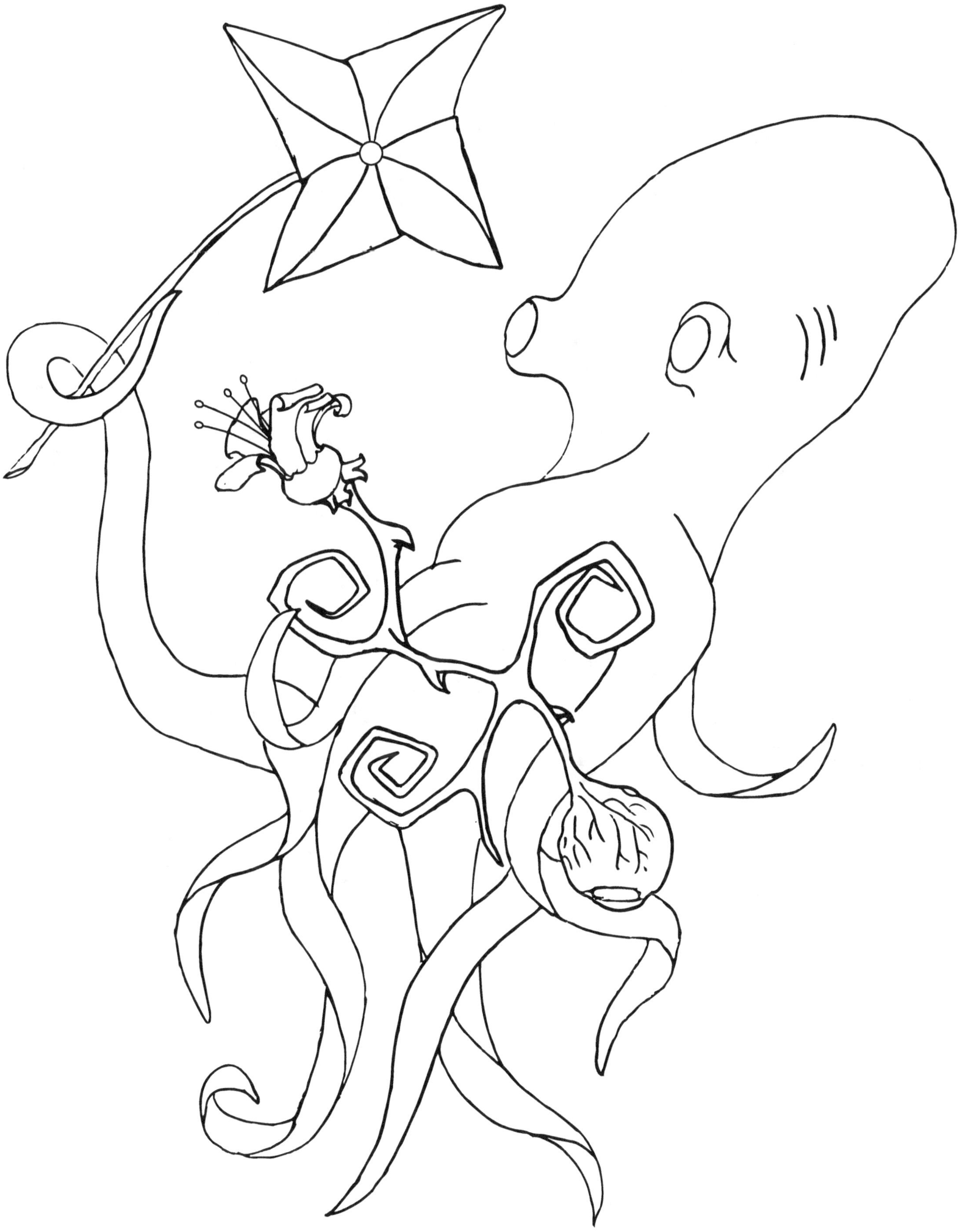

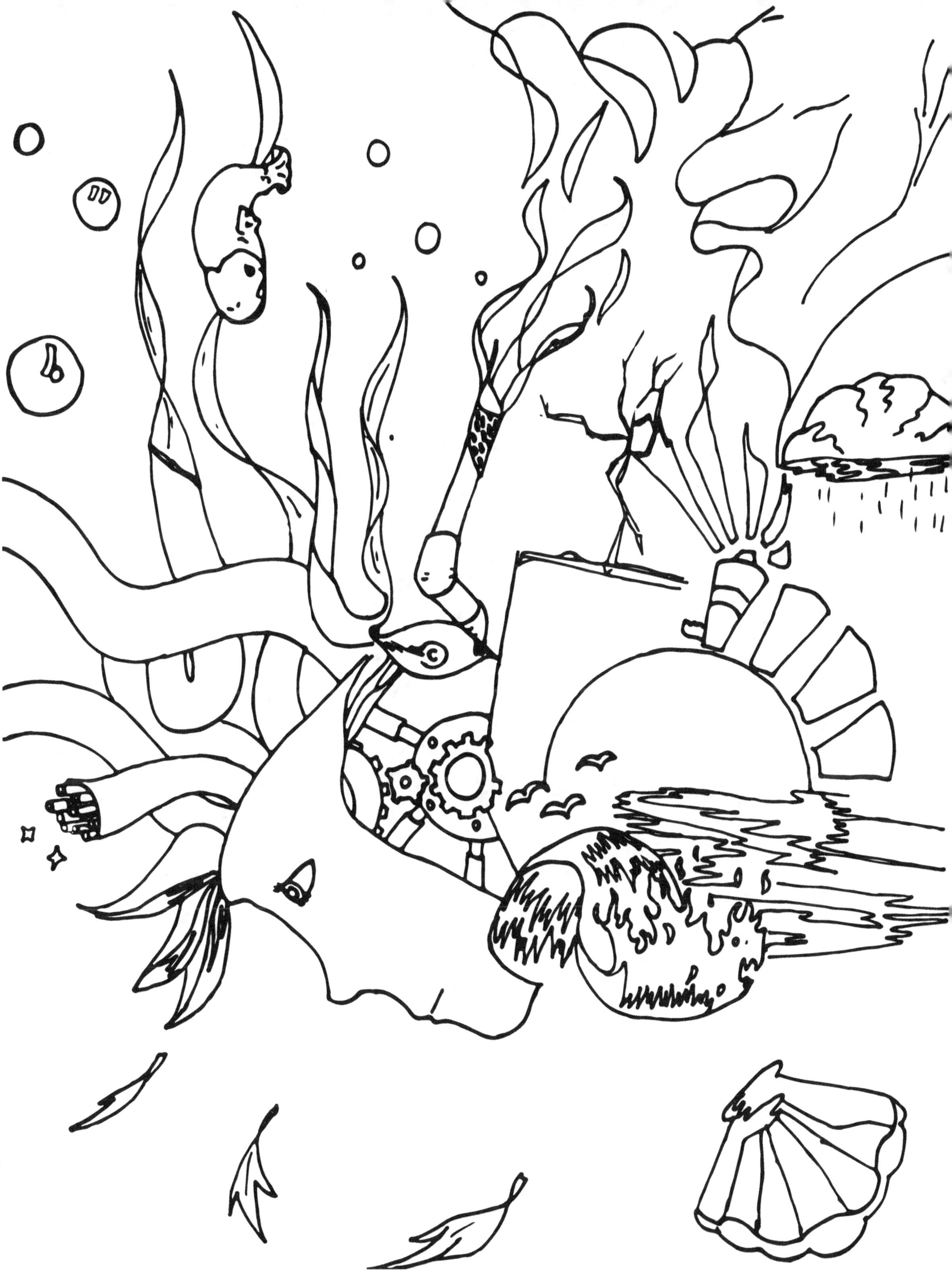

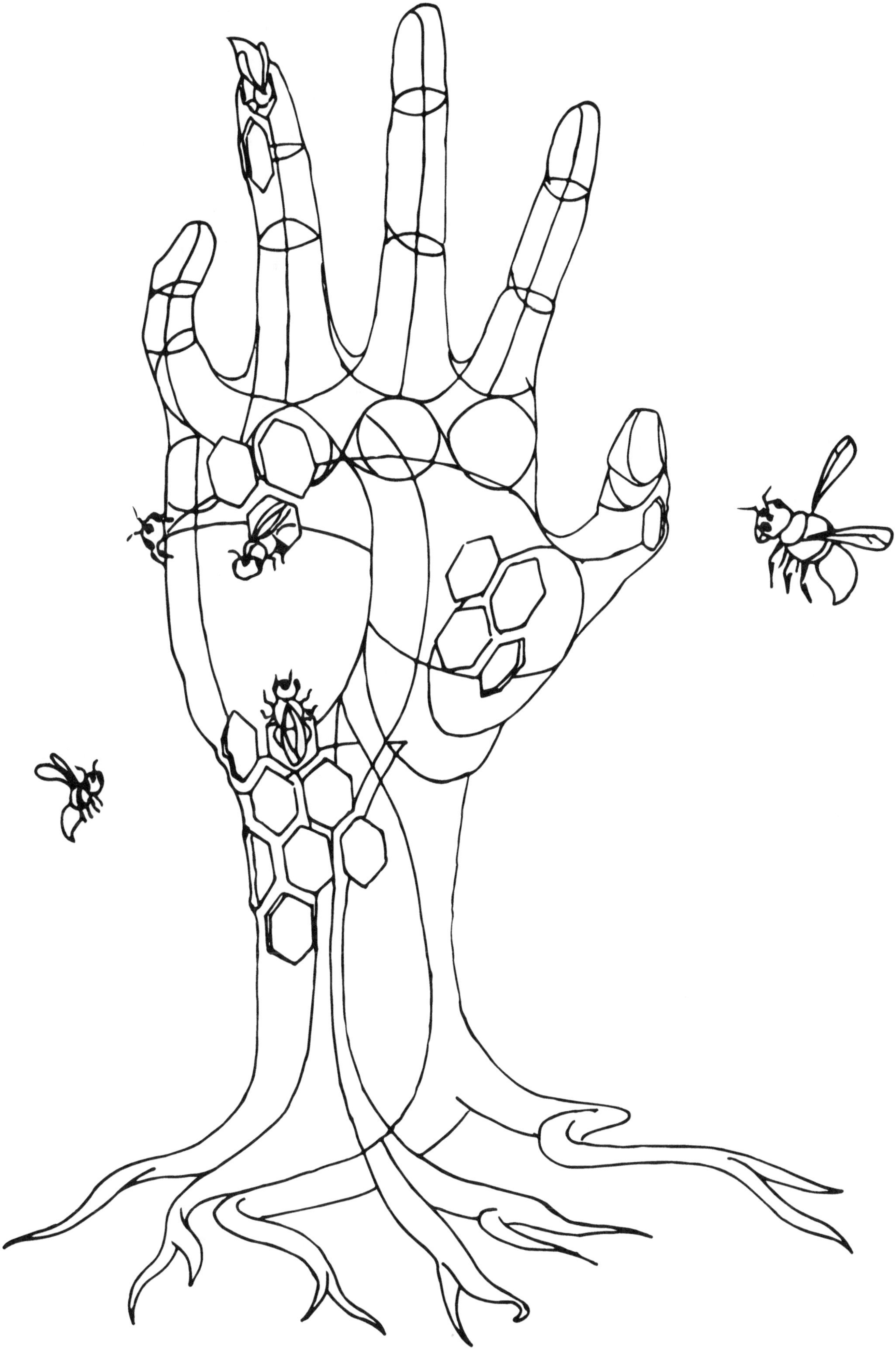

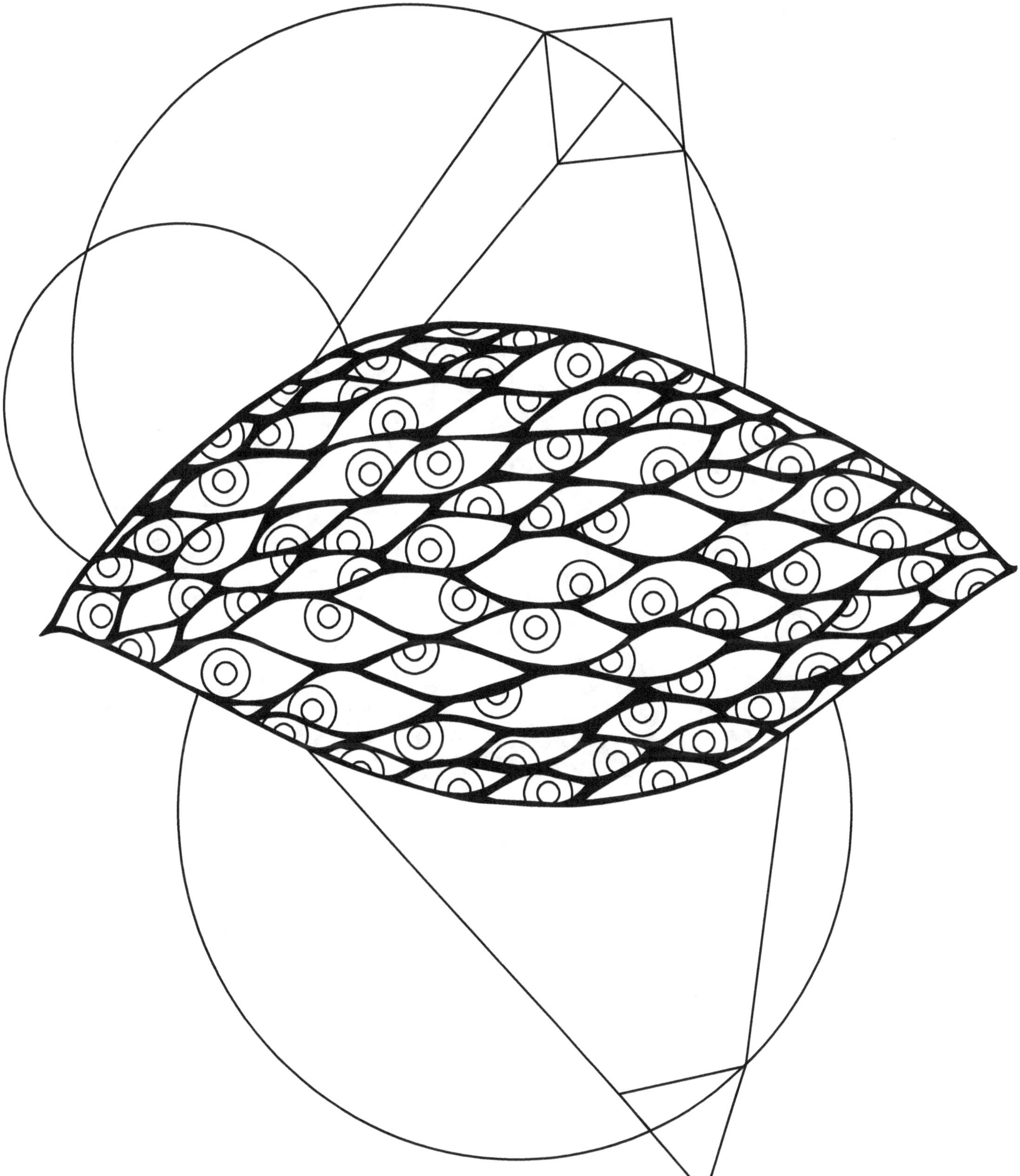

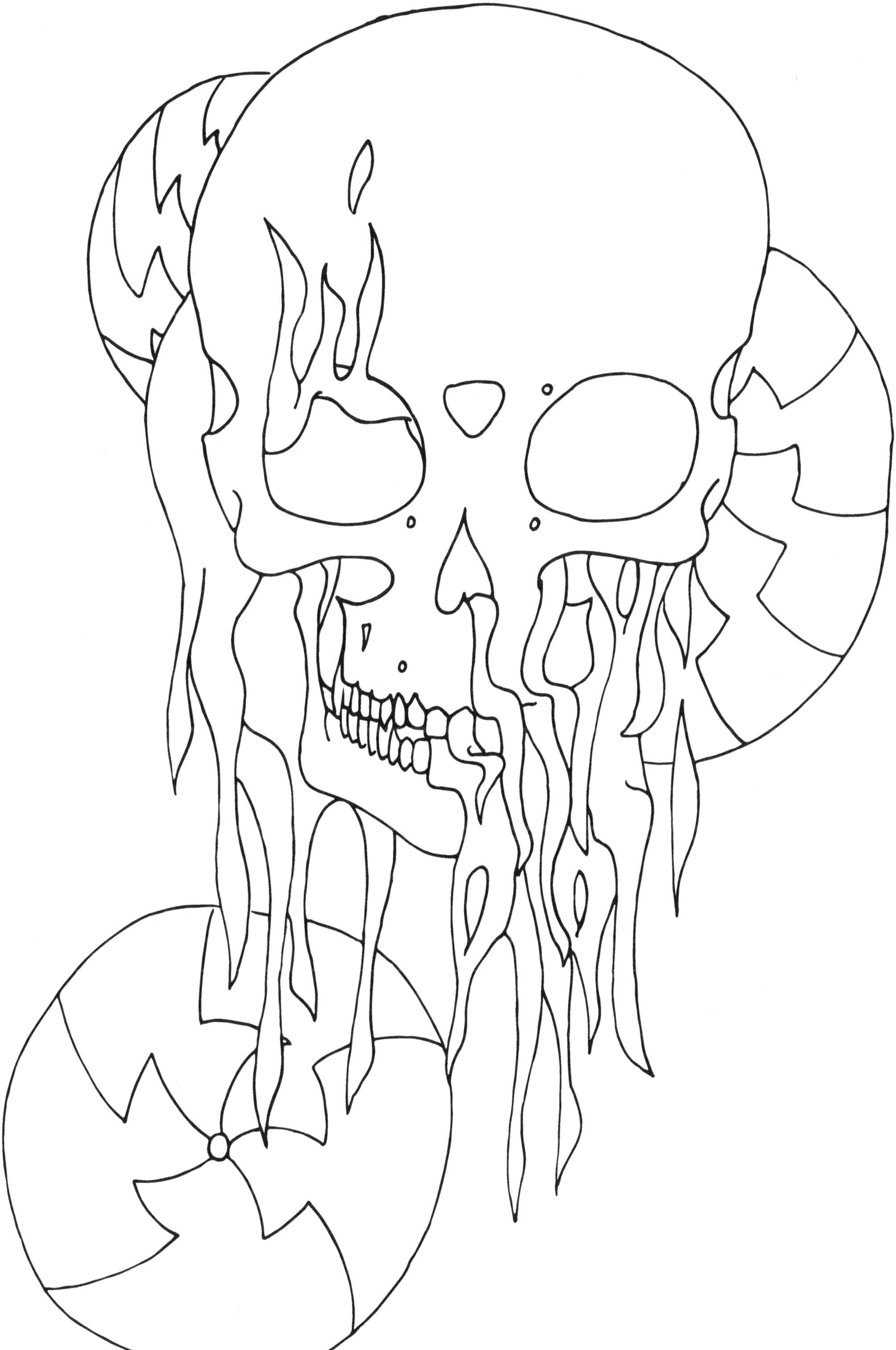

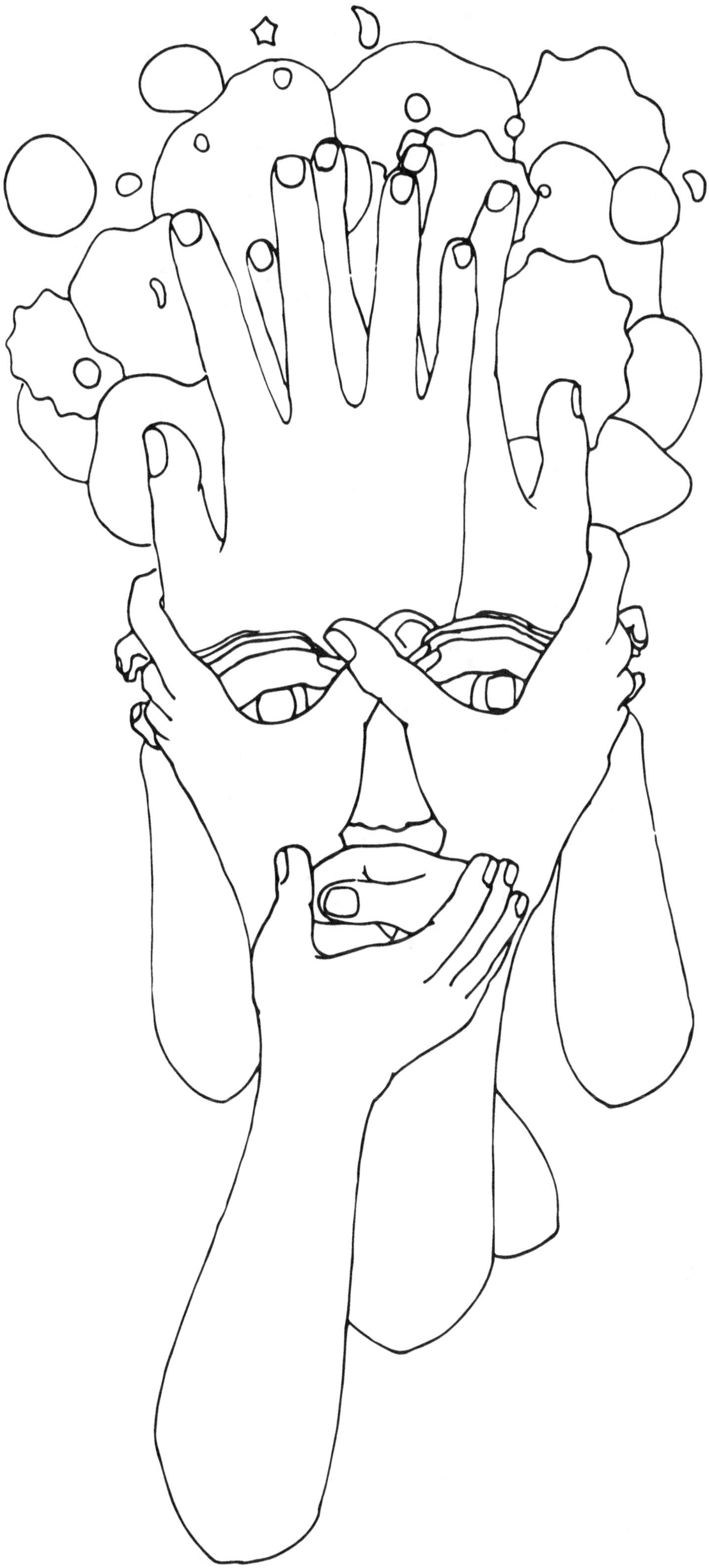

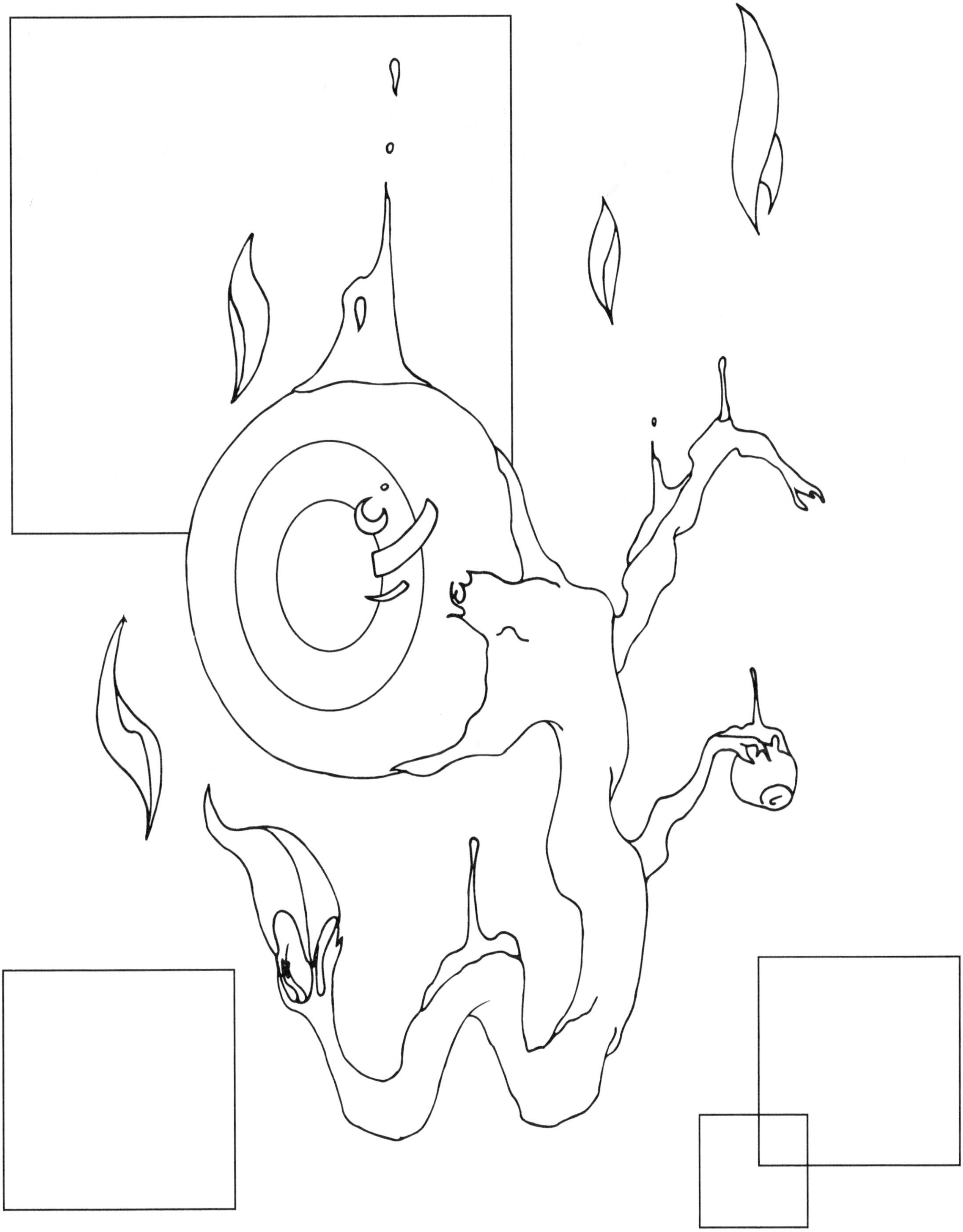

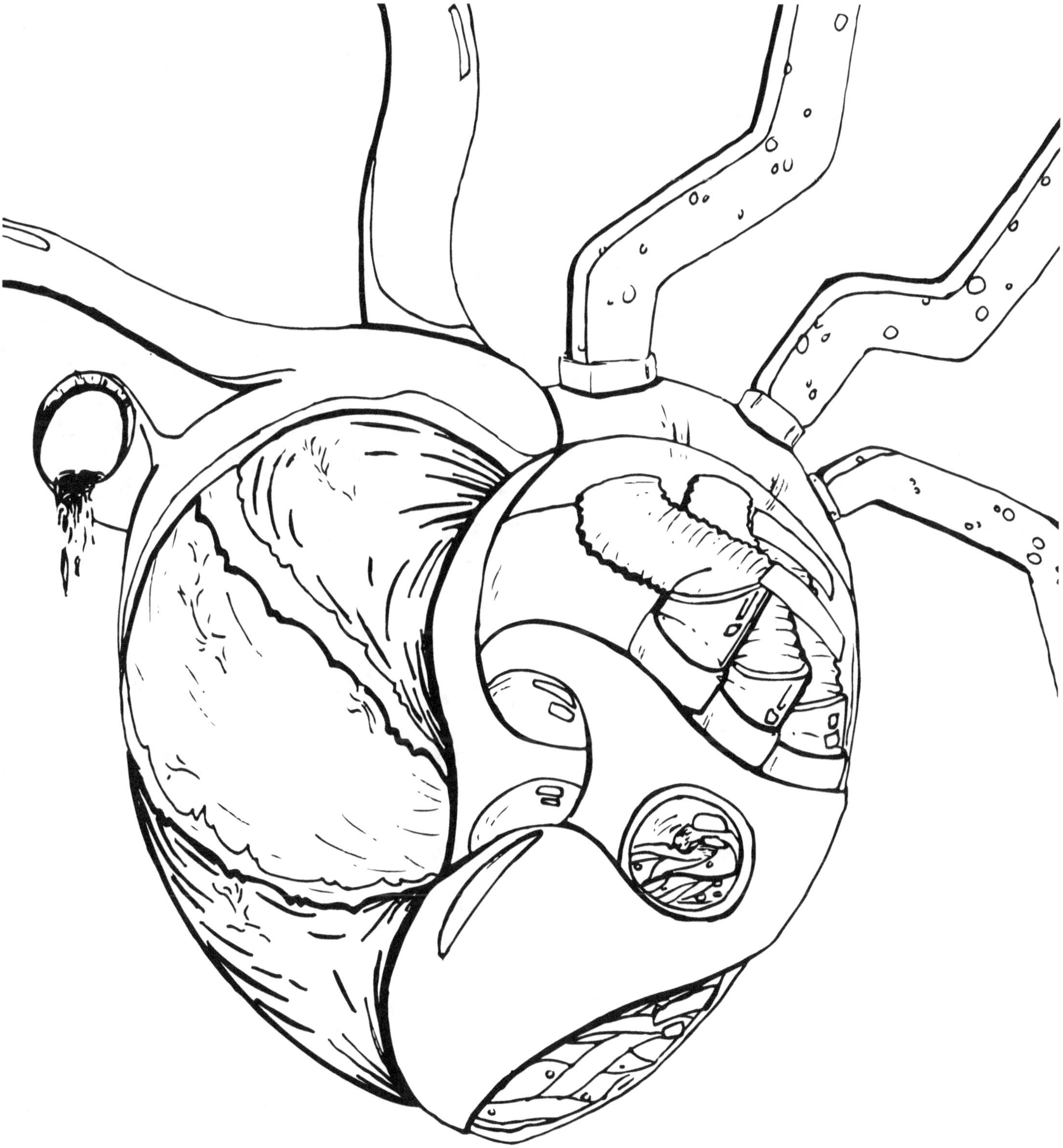

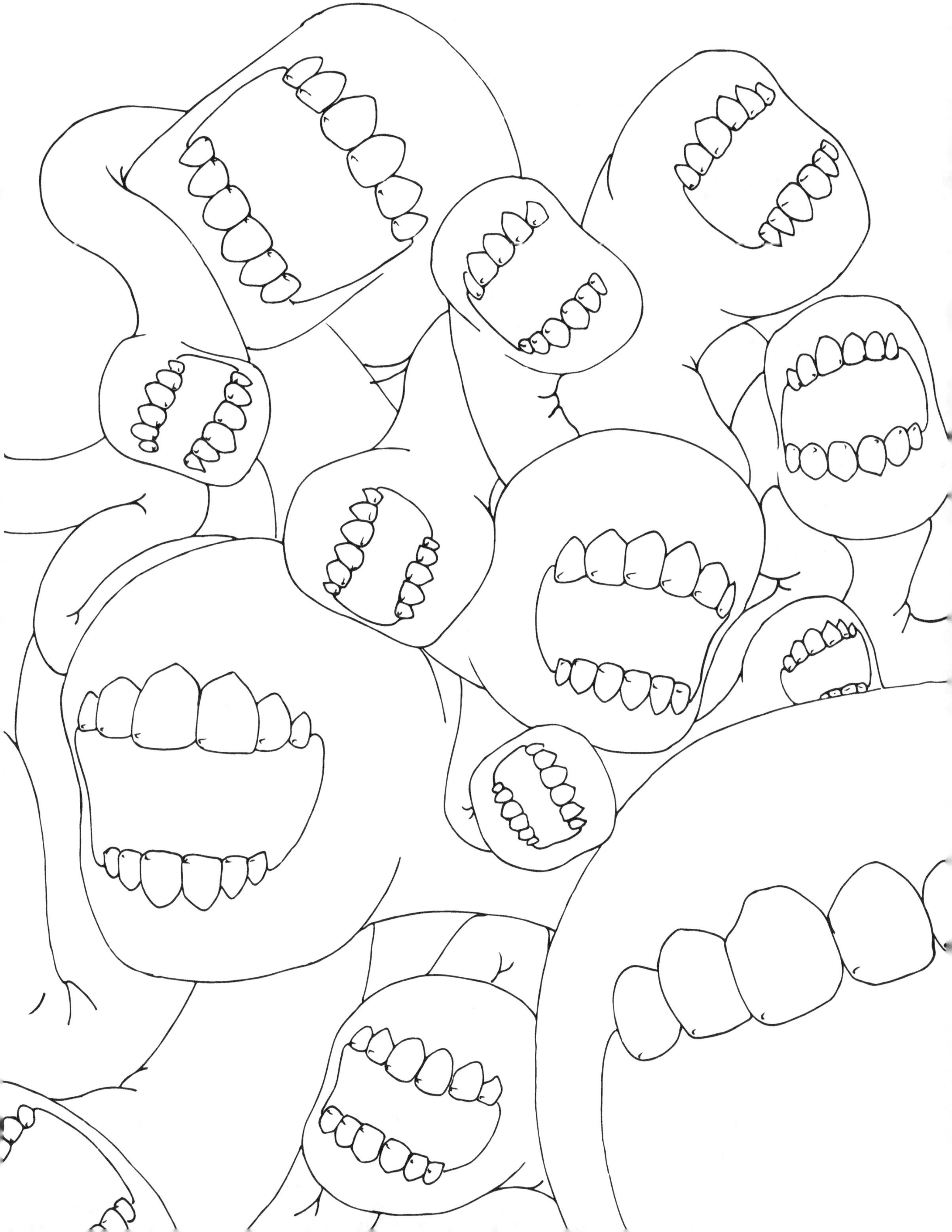

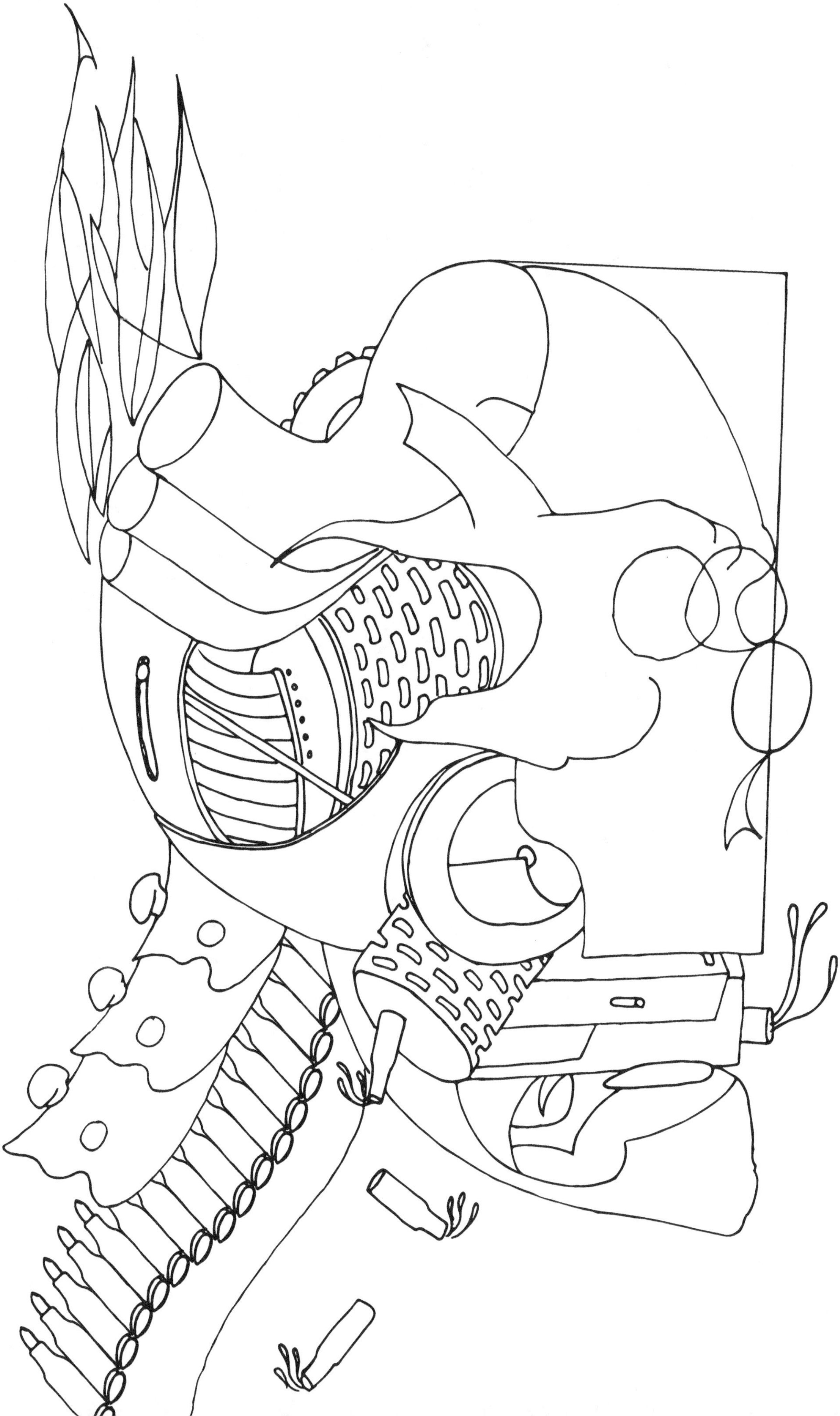

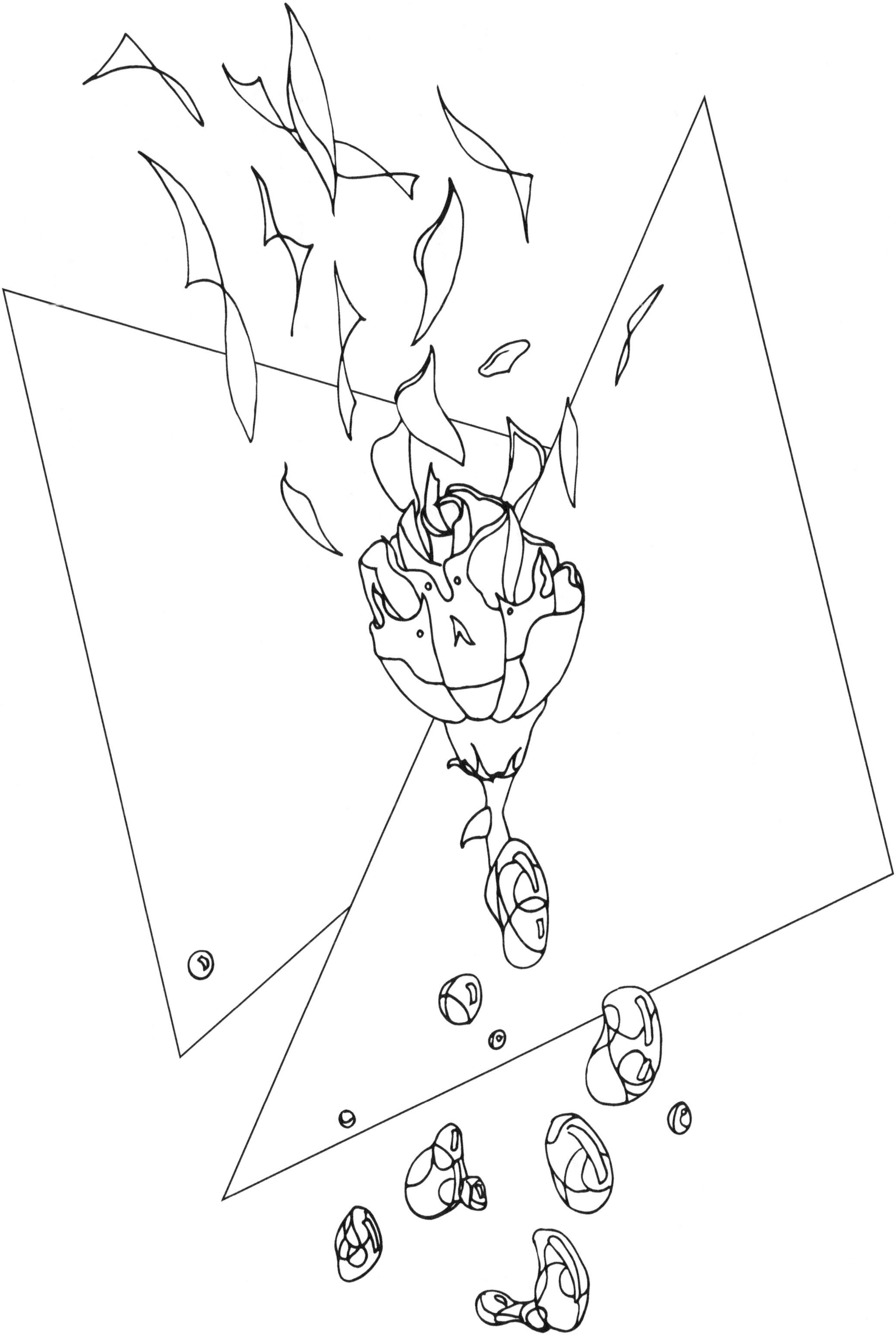

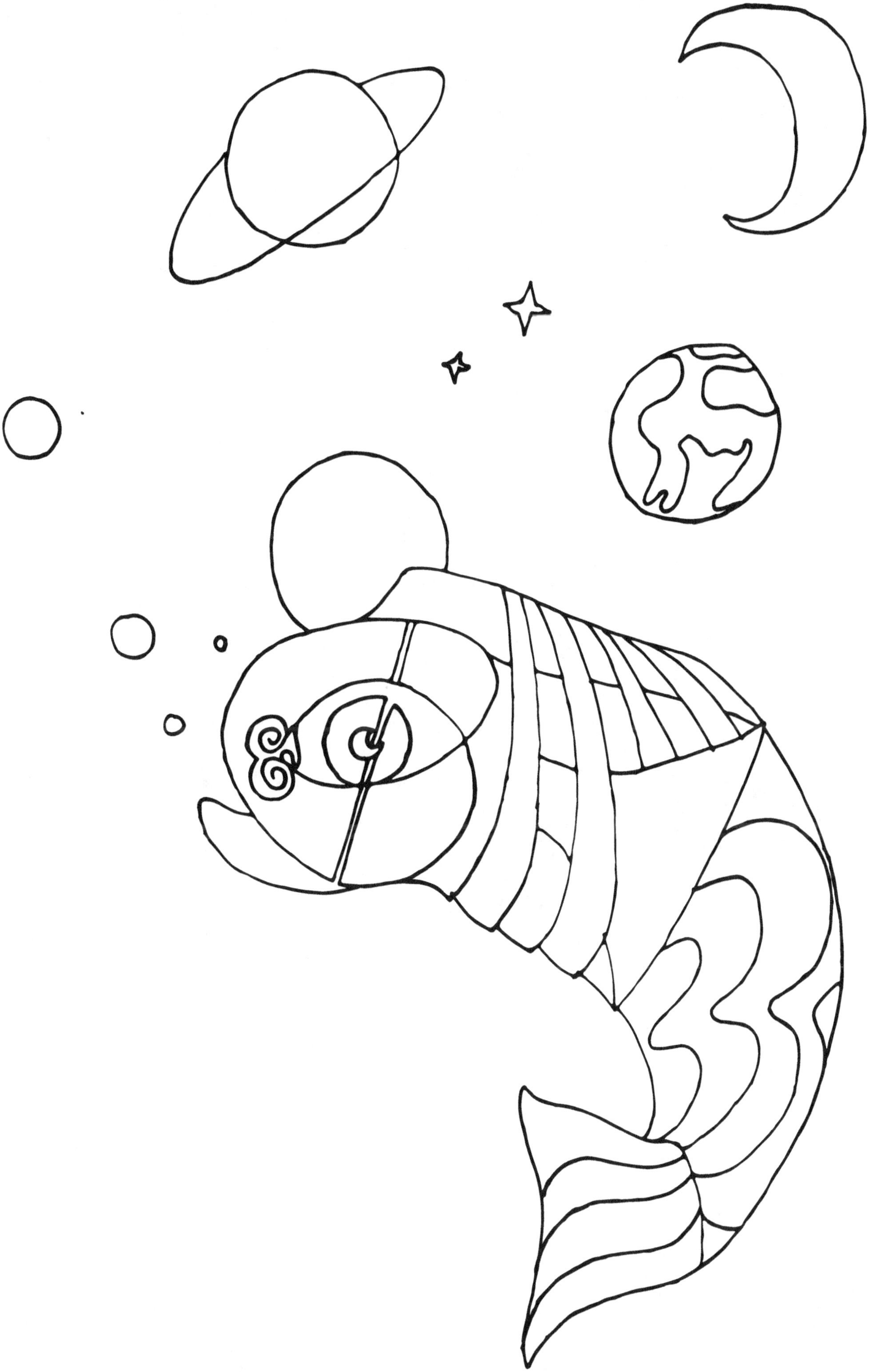

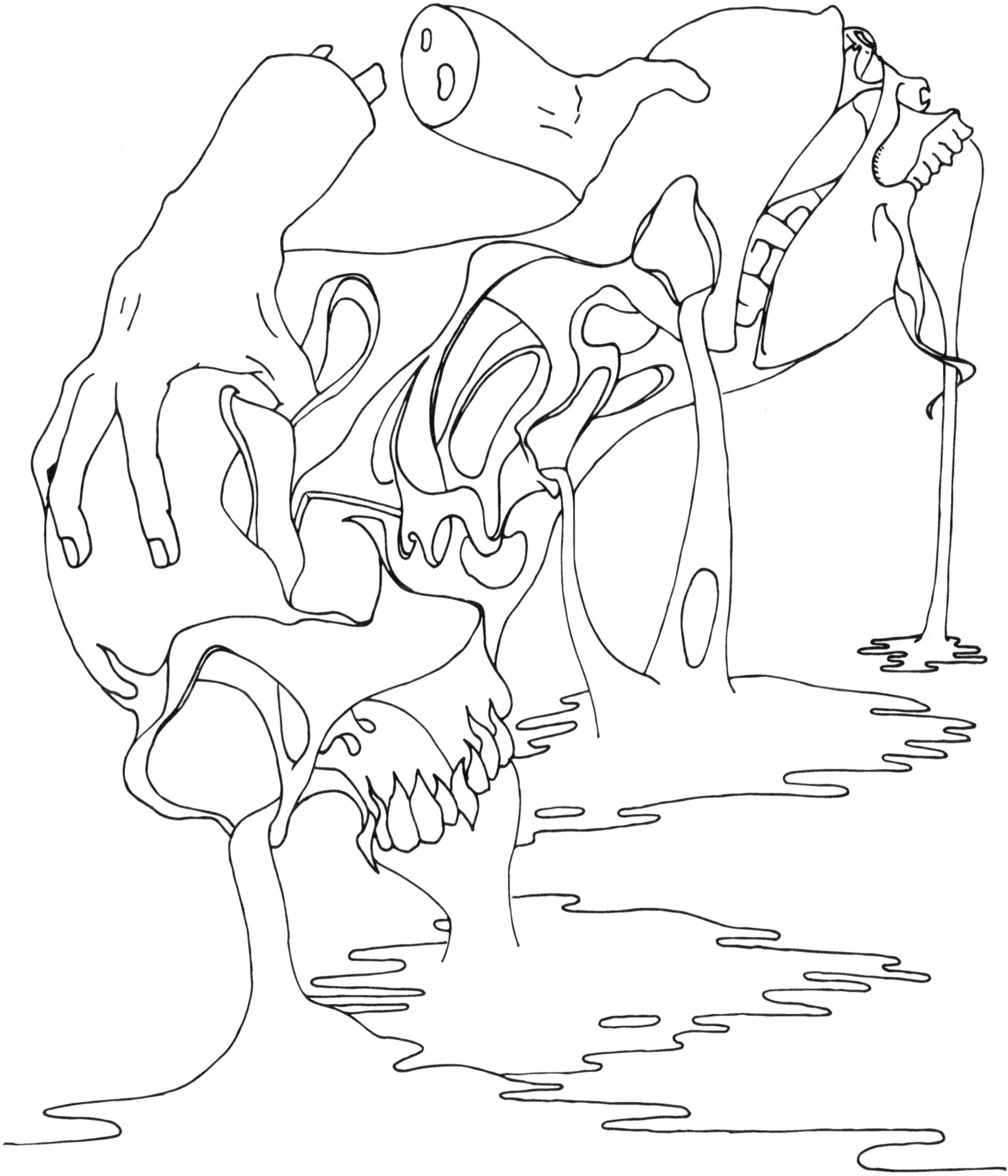

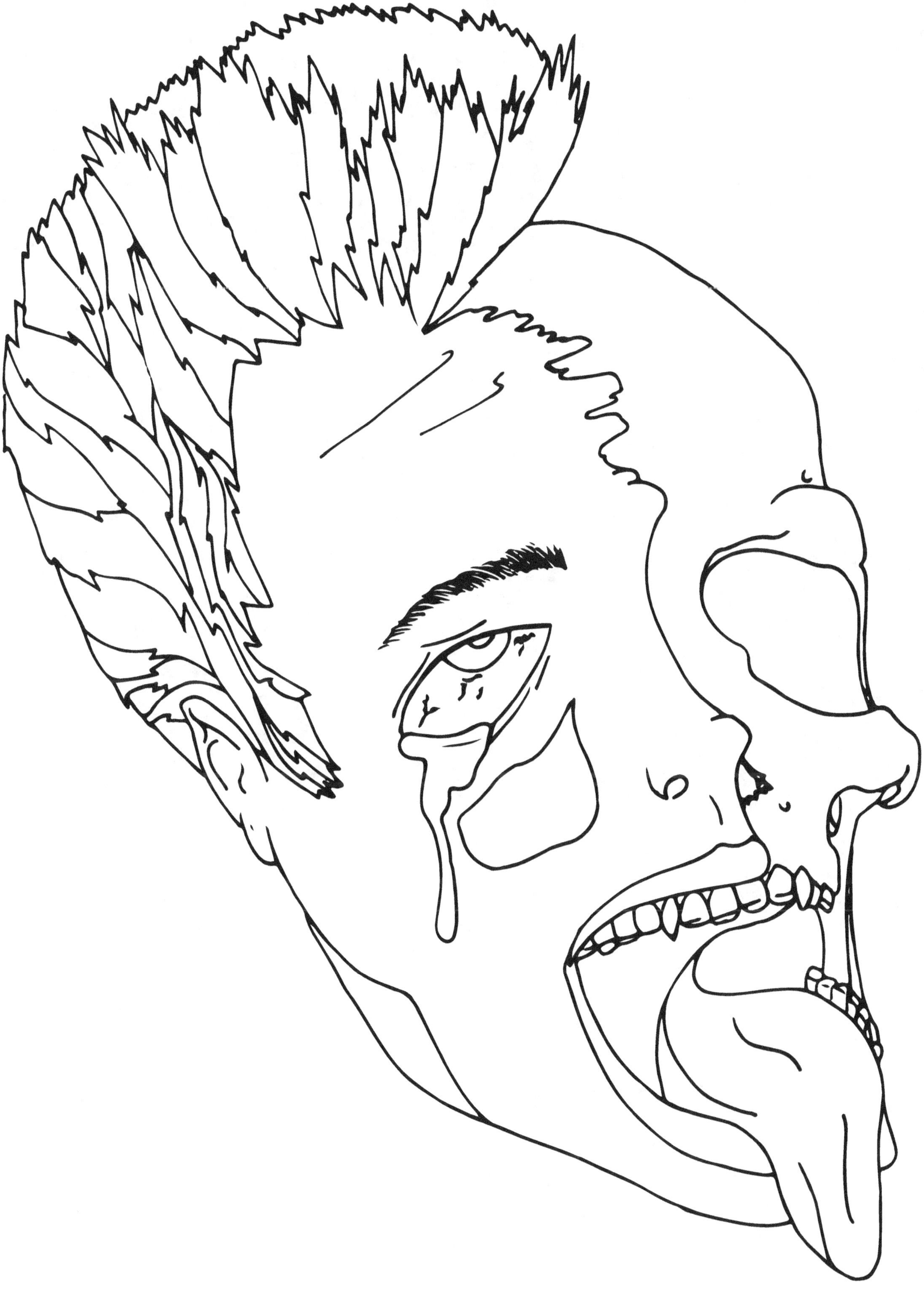

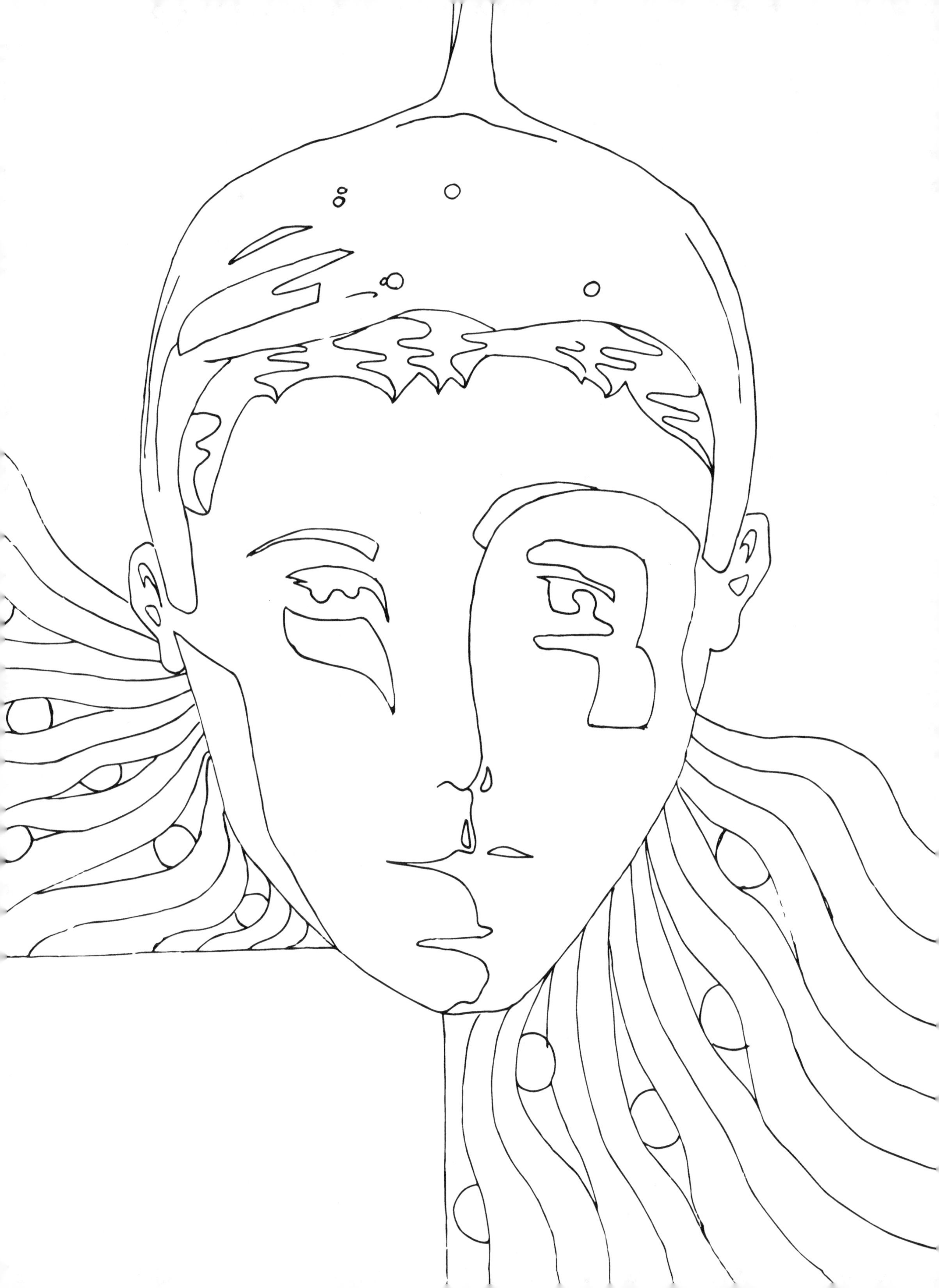

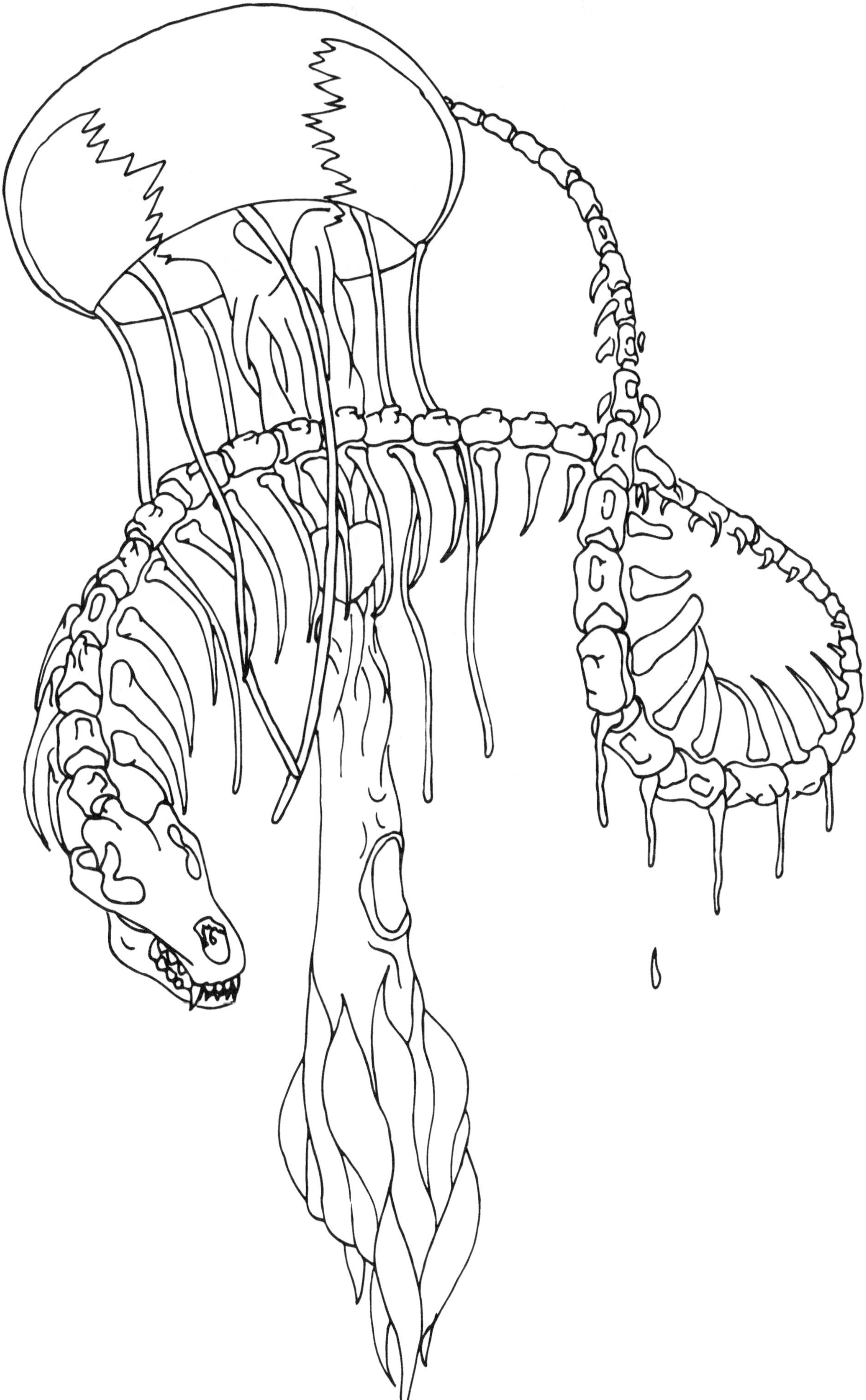

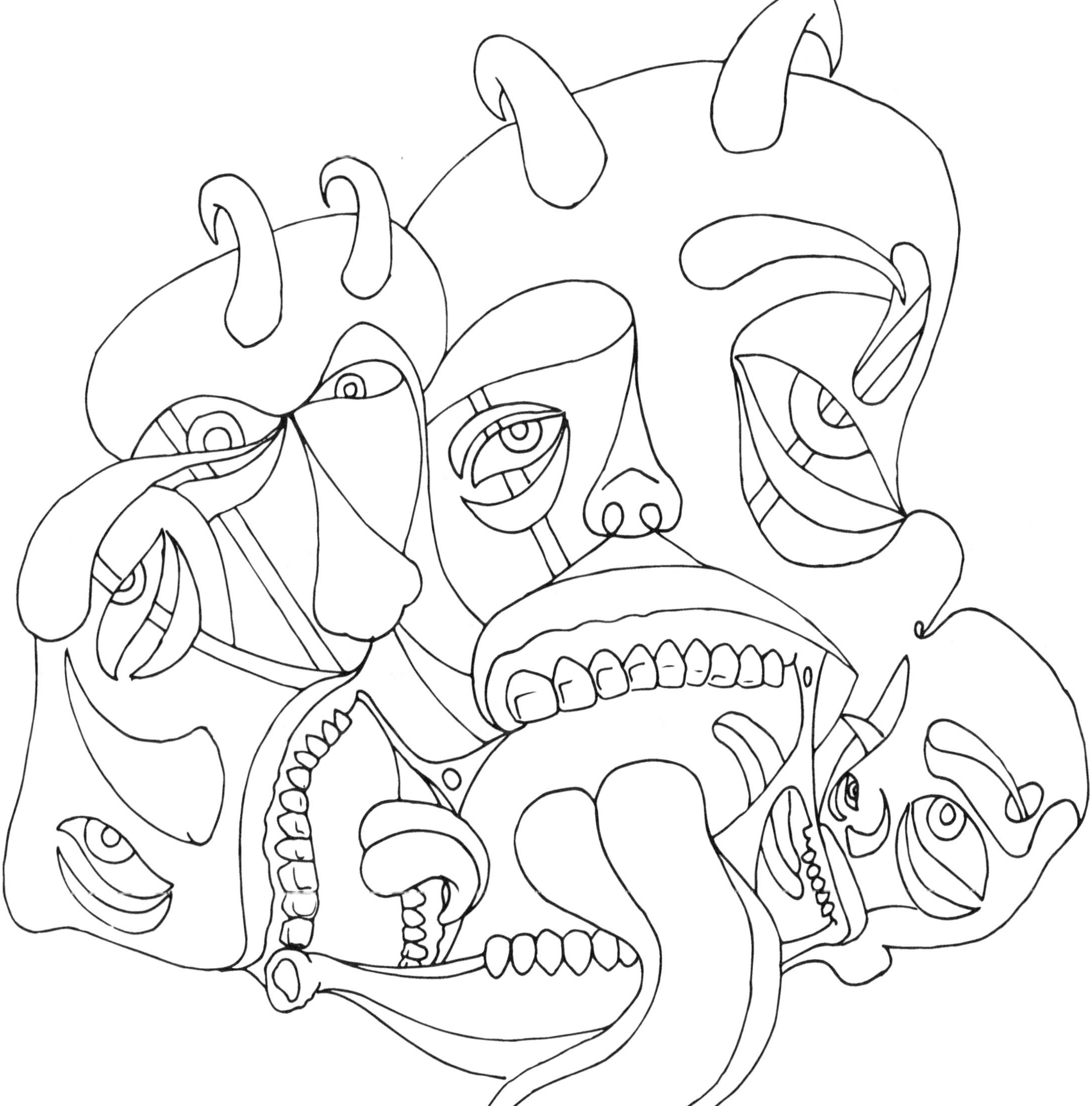

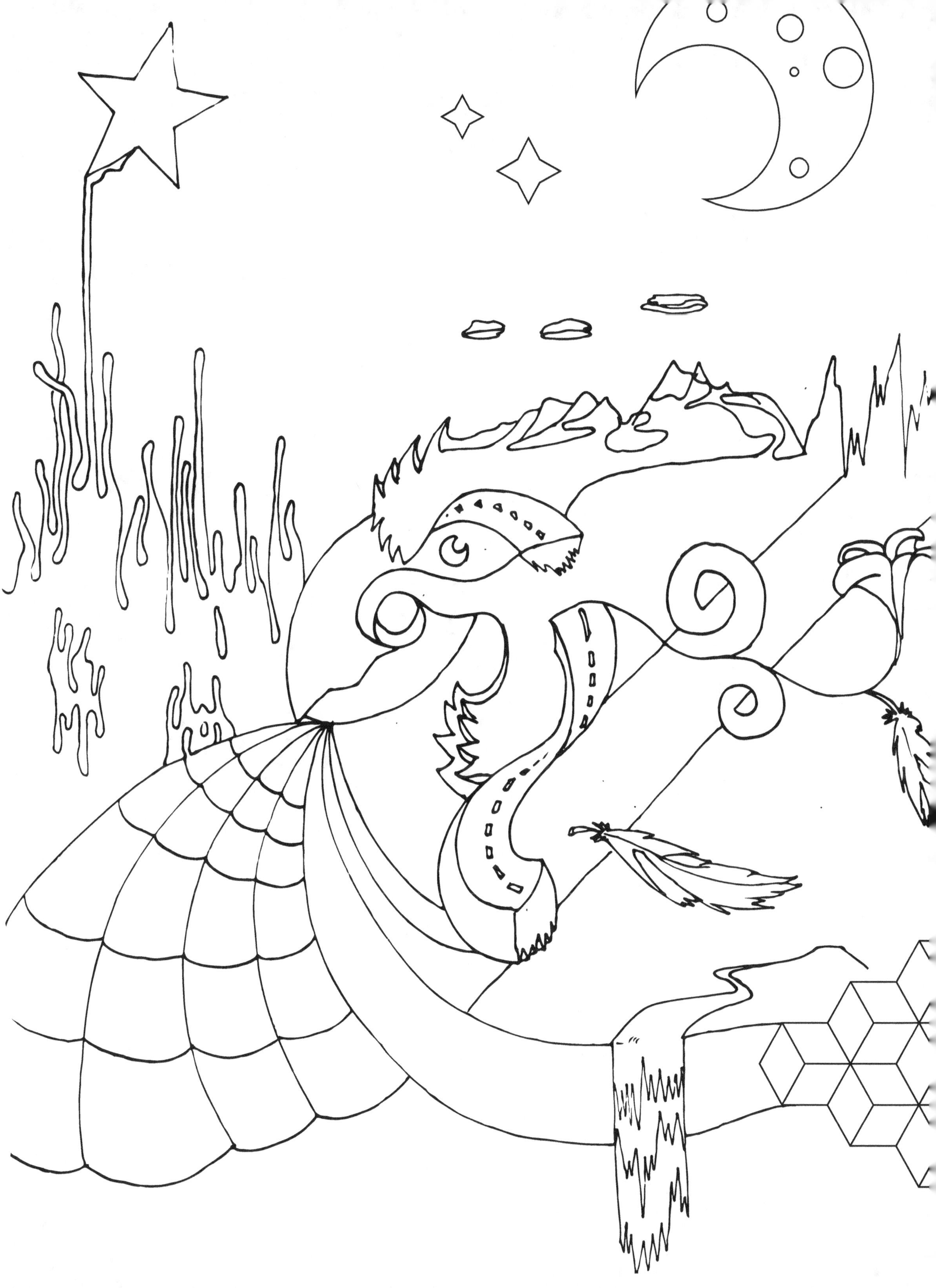

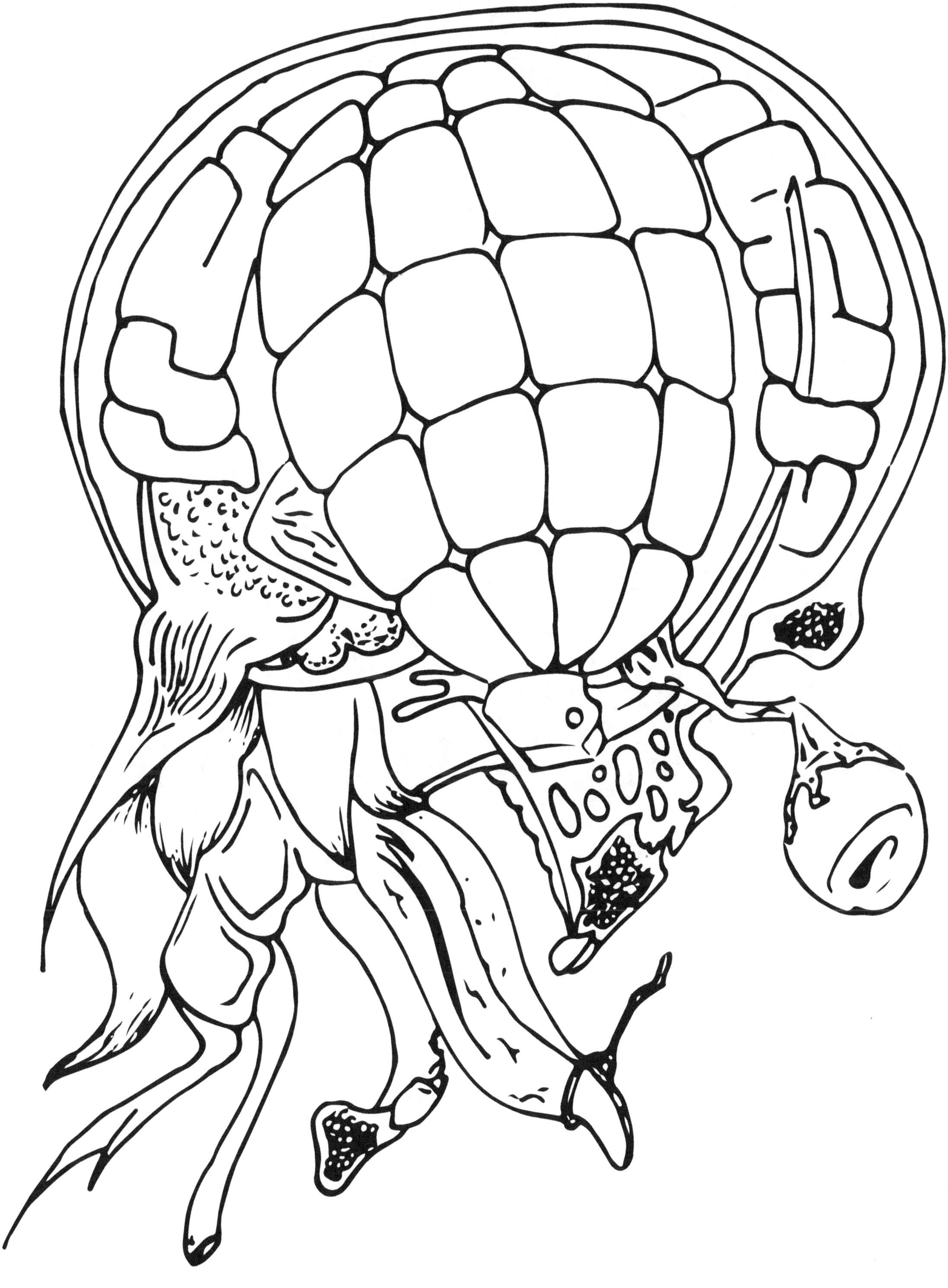

www.ingramcontent.com/pod-product-compliance
Lightning Source LLC
Chambersburg PA
CBHW081134180526
45170CB00008B/3102
9781541142237